All rights reserved.
No part of this book may be
reproduced or used in any manner
without the prior written permission of
the copyright owner, except for the use
of brief quotations in a book review.

This Book of Glitch belongs to:

At first there was only darkness & light,

Black & white,

as it had always been...

...Between
them, as always,
and as old as time

there was a line,

a line in time...

...The very same line
that always was,
just there, in between,
no closer to light than dark,
just in between

as it had always been...

...Dark & Light had different conversations over time,

they spoke about the line, the line as old as time that had always been defined...

...They both remembered there was something more to the line as they looked back in time a Zebra came to mind...

...Neither

could recall a time,
where there had been
no line,

the line as old as time,

...they had always been 3,

as it had always been
and would be...

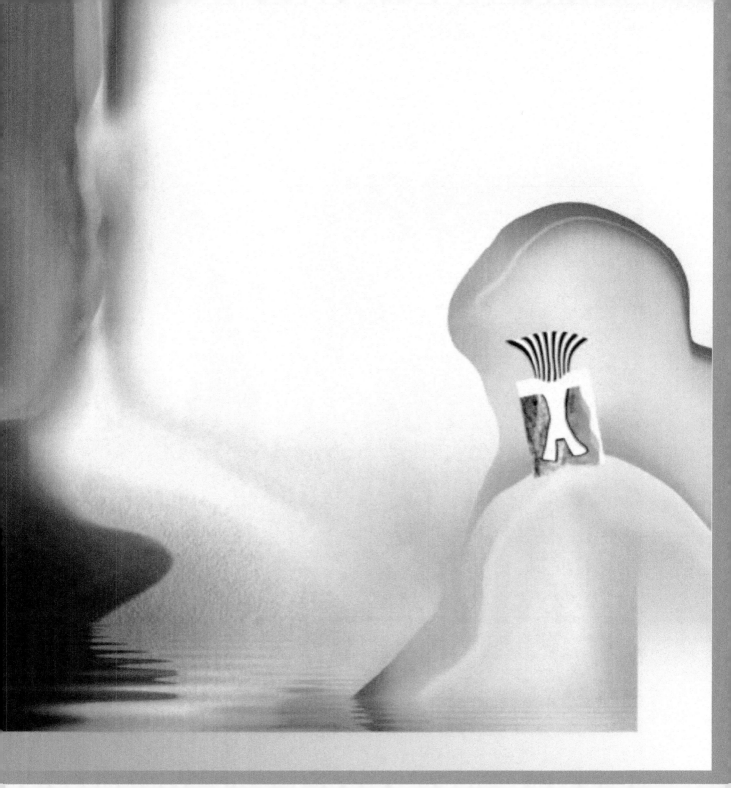

... *Light*

said the line was Black

as it had always said

looking back...

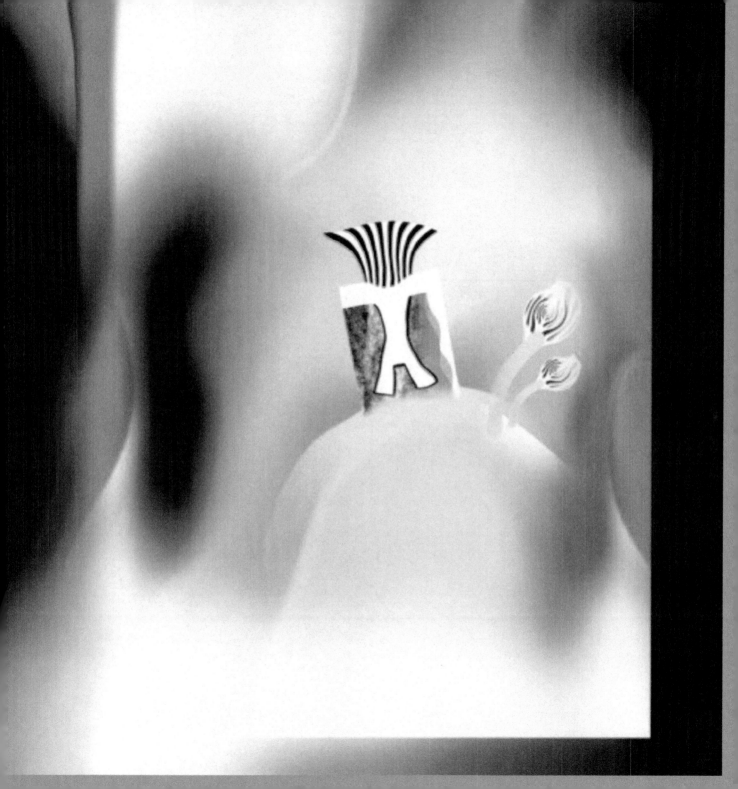

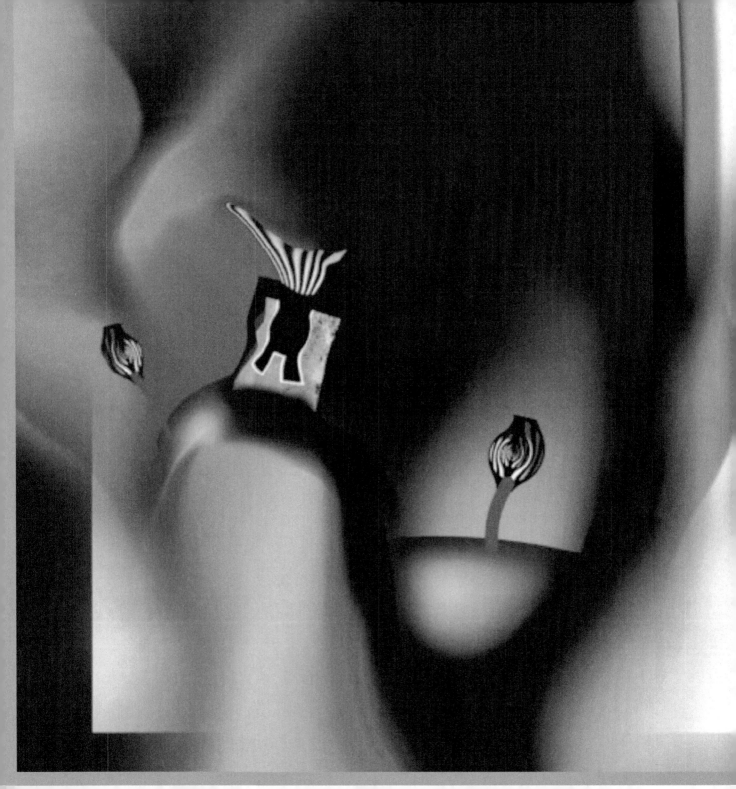

... However

and forever

Dark had seen it,

to be

white,

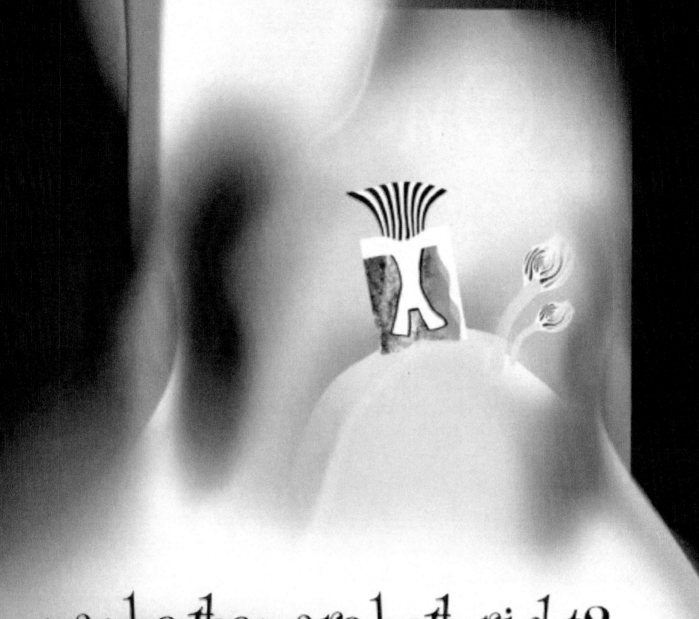

...One thing was understood,
the line that was as old as time
had always been there

as it always had

and always

would...

...A friendly disagreement.
continued over the line
as old as time...

....What
would happen
if there was
no line?

...or if Light or Dark
pushed the line just a little,

the smallest of pushes...
a tease...
a tickle...
maybe a nudge...
Would it budge?

...What if?

what if?

Would it

twitch?

...What is that?

...What can it be?

...The result of all 3 ?

Glitch is born
and Glitch will be,
adventuring on
completely
free.

Glitch is you,
Glitch is me,
Glitch is a combination of the 3.

There
is Black,
there is White,
there is Dark,
there is Light...

...Amazing

things happen

through a   with Light.

Prism

...A Spectrum of colours

beam out from the

white...

Red

Orange

Yellow

Green

Blue

Indigo

Violet

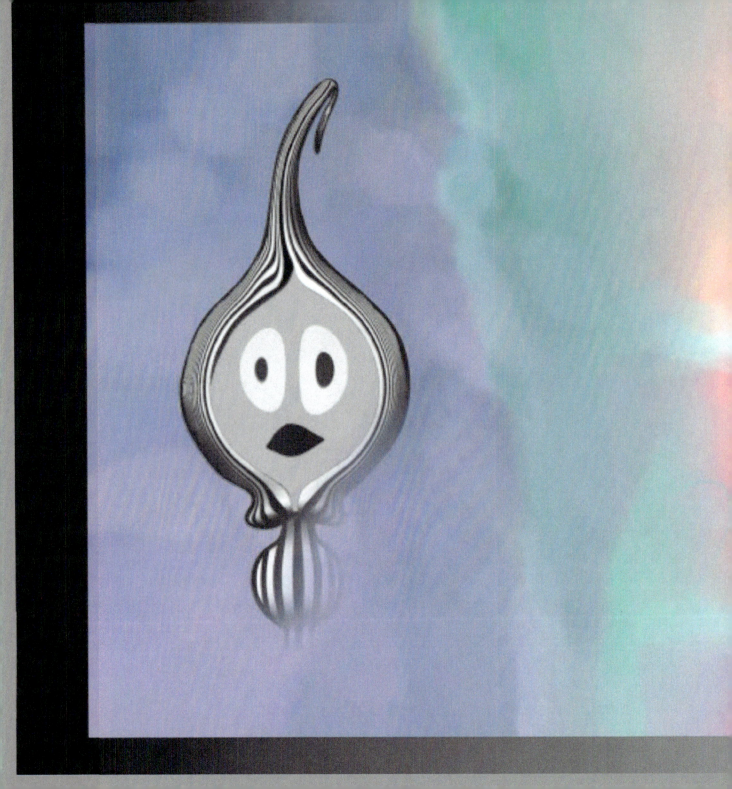

All colours are equal
and each have their space...

...and without each other
there is a strange place.

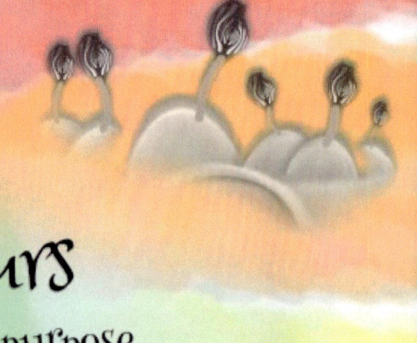

Colours
have purpose
and feelings they entice
but most of all they
really look nice.

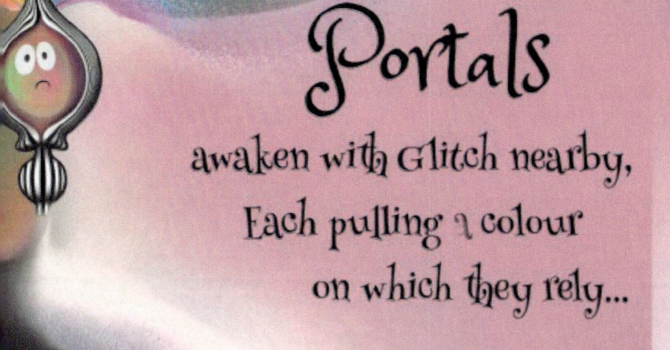

Portals

awaken with Glitch nearby,

Each pulling a colour

on which they rely...

Pathways

to adventure that mistify.

Let's look at the colours and understand why...

Red the Angry cloud,

the Love in our head.

Spontaneous warmth with a seam of dread...

Joyfully vibrant but don't be misled.

Attracting attention

and Caution

instead.

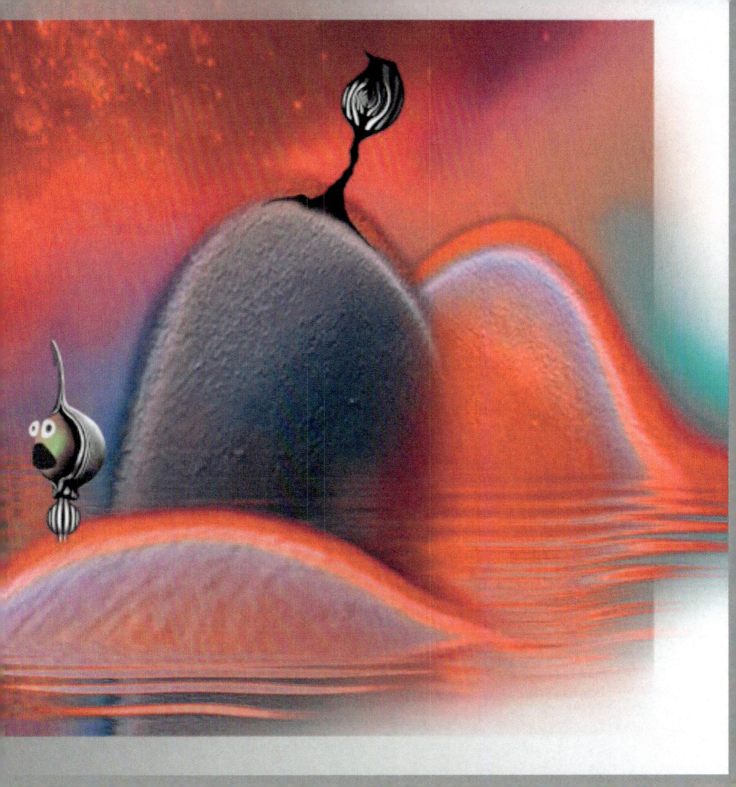

Orange

is joyful
and positively embracing,
Sun shaped warmth,
and a fruit that's amazing.

Orange vest, Orange zest,
Join the quest at
Glitch's behest.

Light must be seen for grass to stay keen,
Grass in a cave has never been seen.

Have you seen all the things
that surround us in Green?
What are they called,
what have
you seen?

Blue

can be Deep,

Strong and Relial

Or as clear as the sky which is undeniable...

Somedays we all feel unsure on what to do,

but it's okay at times to feel a little Blue...

...just be kind to yourself and talk it throug

Indigo

is Chill and full of
Compassion, Confident, harmonious
and seen in Fashion.

The midnight sky with night vision,
Seeing star like jewels that glisten.

Violet

is Noble and Mysteriously Luminous...
...Look at the skylit depths of the Universe.

Memories

nite,
ashing through   Dark & Light.
Glitch gave them happiness
as they
laughed through
the night.

The multicoloured magical zebra was the highlight but we will save that story for another night.

Thank you

Glitch,

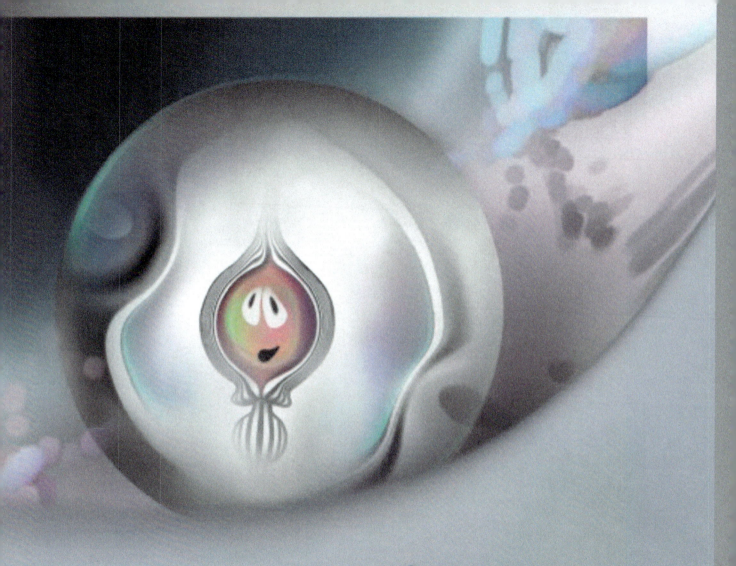

time to sleep tight,
 night, night!!

Printed in Great Britain
by Amazon